The Sound of One Thigh Clapping

Haiku for a Thinner You

MEREDITH CLAIR

WORKMAN PUBLISHING • NEW YORK

Illustrations by Cyril Cabry

Library of Congress Cataloging-in-Publication Data
Clair, Meredith
     The sound of one thigh clapping : haiku for a thinner you /
          by Meredith Clair.
        p. cm
     ISBN 0-7611-3142-6
       1. Haiku, American. 2. Overweight persons—poetry. 3.
     Reducing diets—Poetry. 4. Weight loss—Poetry. I. Title
     PS3603.L345S68 2003   2003057679
     811'.54—dc22

Workman books are available at special discounts when
purchased in bulk for premiums and sales promotions as well
as for fund-raising or educational use. Special editions or
book excerpts can also be created to specification. For details,
contact the Special Sales Director at the address below.

Workman Publishing Company, Inc.
708 Broadway
New York, NY 10003-9555
www.workman.com

Printed in the U.S.A.
First printed: October 2003
10 9 8 7 6 5 4 3 2 1

C
O
N
T
E
N
T
S

For Ertha and the Trio

I am grateful to Jennifer Griffin and her colleagues at Workman Publishing Co. for their wit, talent, and professionalism. I would also like to thank friends and family who reviewed early drafts of the manuscript and listened (over and over) to my tales of Ertha. Most important, I would like to thank Kera Bolonik for her support, her critical eye, and her unflagging enthusiasm about this project.

Let Haiku lead you

out of Hellfatdarkness. Run!

To the Land of Thin.

Before I reached the age of thirty, I had tried just about every diet known to humankind. Each promised a quick and easy fix—all I needed to do was shell out some cash for pills, powders, shakes, or protein bars and wait the prescribed period for the fat to "melt away." When one diet didn't work, which was usually the case, there was always another "must try" scheme beckoning from the covers of magazines at the grocery check-out. There was the All-Cabbage diet, the Eat Only Bacon and Cheese and Lose Weight! diet (a personal favorite), the No Protein and Carbs at the Same Time diet, the This Shake Will Fill You Up as Much as a Meal diet, the intriguing 30 Pounds in 30 Days diet. . . . Though each was alluring in its own way, I knew before I started that all were doomed to fail. I suppose I took for granted that weight loss was something that I would always strive for but would never achieve.

My most recent diet adventure was not unlike group therapy. The leader of the group, a woman

THINSPIRATION

"A man's home is his White Castle."

named Ertha, had the charisma of a southern Baptist tent-revival preacher, all hellfire and brimstone, emboldened by her unwavering conviction that her cause was just. We, her fearless regulars, clung to her words as if they were so many morsels of fat-free manna fallen from the heavens.

Ertha spoke in parables and often didn't make sense to anyone—even to the ever-growing group of veteran attendees. In the times when I was able to follow her, it seemed that most of her lessons pointed to the same deceptively simple truth, that craving is the root of all suffering. Ertha devoted a great deal of time to explaining this concept in various ways and often relied on diagrams to drive the point home.

Each meeting began with a brief consideration of her quote of the day, usually something pithy and confounding, like "Self-Esteem = Sodium." No one knew what she meant by this, but we all had a sense that this quote, along with countless others that were equally, if not more, perplexing, had a deeper meaning. We all felt that if we contemplated Ertha's bits of wisdom, finally the door to the Land of Thin (as she called it) would spring open. So we returned, week after week, weighing in, commiserating, pondering, and peering through the darkness for occasional glimpses of the wonders that awaited the truly diligent.

Ertha encouraged us to simplify our lives and be vigilant in our quest for Thin. So inspired were her lessons that, afterward, I would shudder at the mere sight of some poor unenlightened soul biting into a greasy slice of pizza. Under Ertha's expert tutelage, we meditated on our ideal version of ourselves. We slowly altered our bad eating habits by imagining ourselves thin and happy, biting daintily into a Gardenburger. We were warned that by yielding to the empty, fleeting promises of

THINSPIRATION

"Man cannot live by bread alone,
unless it's slathered in butter."

Frappuccinos, fried chicken, and
Krispy Kreme doughnuts, however
tempting, we would find ourselves
further from our goal weight. We
had to empty our minds (and our
stomachs) of such desires.

Ertha acknowledged that in order
to achieve Thin, we would have to
sacrifice—to accept that we would be
forever burdened by the melancholy
of knowing that we couldn't eat
whatever we wanted to. Yet Ertha
was confident that such knowledge
would ultimately free us from the
dizzying cycle of weight gain and

loss (and gain and loss and gain and loss . . .) that had plagued most of us throughout our lifetimes.

Then one evening, as I stood waiting to step onto the scale before my Monday-night meeting, it dawned on me. Ertha, with all her quirky pearls of wisdom, was actually a Zen master, cloaked in the guise of an ordinary citizen! She had the inner calm and perseverance of Buddha leading a group of young practitioners along the road to Nirvana.

The more I thought about it, the more it all started to make sense. Ertha's methods, which involved cutting out the fat in our thinking and stripping down to the bare essentials, reminded me of haiku, the Japanese poetry form often associated with Zen practice. To write a good haiku, one must pare down, economize, and make sacrifices. Similarly, Ertha taught us that to achieve success in the weight-loss context, we must select our foods carefully, measure each morsel, decrease portions, and ask ourselves tough questions like, "Is that Cinnabon really necessary?" Steeped as I was in Ertha's Zen-style weight-loss philosophy, I soon found myself jotting down haiku poems in the margins of the newspaper as I com-muted to work in the morning. And I was losing weight!

What follows is my attempt to share the insights I have gleaned from Ertha in the form of these haiku that she unwittingly inspired. Be warned, haiku poetry, like diet-

THINSPIRATION

"A bird in the hand is worth 2 Points."

(Calculation based on 4 oz. North American variety, feathers removed.)

THINSPIRATION

"It is no use crying over spilt skim milk."

ing, is often very confusing—even contradictory. Just when you think you understand where the author is going, she changes direction, leaving you completely perplexed. The essential truth of dieting, if one can distill it to its bikini-waxed essence, is paradox. How else can you explain fatfree ice cream, or a person losing weight while eating nothing but cheese, eggs, and meat? By embracing the seeming contradictions, and by accepting that there is no "right" answer to vexing questions like "Why am I destined to weigh more than all my friends?" you will begin to see the lite at the end of the tunnel. As we all know, the true nature of self-image and weight loss is as complex and multilayered as an onion. It is my hope that, by contemplating the following words, you will be able to peel that onion, layer by layer, until you are left with a much smaller, less filling onion. And that, after all, is the whole Point.

THE TAO OF DOUGH: THE EMPTY PROMISE OF CARBOHYDRATES

CHAPTER ONE

Like any good Zen master, Ertha began our journey by warning us about the primary stumbling blocks that we would have to overcome if we were ever to reach our ultimate goal, Enlightenupment: that blissful, weightless state known only to the most persistent. Ertha referred to these obstacles as The Four Evil

No-no's: Temptation, Sloth, Jealousy, and Weakness.

Temptation is perhaps the most vexing obstacle, surrounded as we are by fast-food joints, pizza parlors, and shops full of brightly colored confections. How often we find ourselves heading into the Burger King drive-through, like moths to the flame broiler! Ertha spoke freely of her own demons, such as chicken-fried steak slathered in milk gravy; whipped potatoes and butter; pecan pie warmed in a skillet full of bacon grease and served with a generous side of schlag. But Ertha was care-

THINSPIRATION

"Nothing eaten, nothing gained."

ful to instruct that, although we may occasionally give in to Temptation, we must never let it get the best of us if we ever hope to reach the Land of Thin. We must view each grocery store aisle and every restaurant menu as we would the fields of Normandy after World War II—lovely on the outside but riddled with hidden dangers.

How can we survive the ordeal? Ertha wisely explained that the first step in avoiding peril is identifying and embracing the threat. Give in to the Temptation, consider how the sugary or fattening "treat" makes you feel, and then consider how quickly the sensation passes, leaving you alone, crying into empty muffin cups.

Chocolate passes

too quickly over the tongue,

preferring the hips.

Sweet little Goldfish,

always a hit at parties.

Carbohydrate trap.

In the checkout line

I hear the chocolate bars

calling to me. "Yes!"

As a child, I thought

Keebler Elves were innocent.

The folly of youth!

Mrs. Butterworth

beckons with syrupy smiles.

The evil temptress!

Sara Lee puzzles

over her sudden weight gain.

A pound cake, indeed.

Double cheeseburger,

French fries, and a Shamrock Shake.

Glimpses of Heaven.

Visions of Moon Pies

dancing on a custard beach.

Blood sugar is low.

Fond memories of

Hidden Valley Ranch, where I

last saw my waistline.

Seconds on the lips—

and a lifetime on the hips,

thighs, and upper arms.

Praise to the DoveBar!

Little messenger of peace

enrobed in chocolate.

A pang of regret

for having SuperSized it?

Just indigestion.

Lose inches with lard…!

Fight fat with peanut butter…!

The alarm clock sounds.

Thank you, Buffalo,

for the memories, the wings,

and the extra pounds.

But these burgers are

so small, how bad could they be?

The White Castle Myth.

Just ask Mrs. Smith.

Behind every good pie is

a whole lotta fat.

Sweet figgy pudding—

consumed by all the English.

Dowdy? No wonder.

So sweet. So creamy.

Yet so diabolical.

Dulce de Leche.

It's just "water weight,"
though "milk shake weight"
would seem to
be more accurate.

This Filet-O-Fish

is neither fish nor filet.

And yet, I eat it.

The Quarter Pounder

must weigh more than they let on.

Never trust a clown.

CHAPTER TWO

CHOPPING WOOD, CARRYING WATER: THE CHALLENGE OF EXERCISE

Difficult though it may be, resisting Temptation is only the beginning. Early in our journey, Ertha instructed us that we could never hope to reach the Land of Thin if we refused to get off the couch.

Ertha herself was quite athletic and spent many a meeting describing her daily exercise routine—the thought of which left most of us confused, awestruck, and a bit intimidated. Indeed, despite the proliferation of fancy gyms and the new Yoga Chic, many of us find Sloth (second of the Four Evil No-no's) to pose the most formidable roadblock on the Path to Thin.

Ertha was careful to teach us that we cannot jump into a strenuous exercise routine without sufficient preparation, lest we end up

THINSPIRATION

"You can lead a horse to water,

but you can't make it drink

eight glasses a day."

pulling a groin muscle on the StairMaster and spending two weeks recovering with the "help" of our dubious friend Russell Stover.

No, one must prepare for exercise as one would for battle—arming oneself with the proper clothing, goggles, an ample supply of water, and good, sturdy shoes.

Ertha suggested that we start with the basics: Take the steps instead of the elevator! Lunge while vacuuming! Do deep knee bends while cleaning dust bunnies from under the sofa! Before we knew it, we had moved on to an entirely new level, a province hitherto occupied only by the most daring, the most limber, and Jane Fonda.

Who could have guessed that

our Chrissy would turn out to

be the Thighmaster?

Sweating at the gym,

I wonder why I bother.

Liposuction works.

"One! and Two! and Three!"

Look at those silly creatures

bouncing up and down.

Buns of Steel abound.

Airport metal detectors

in state of chaos.

Rationalizing,

I stop at Wendy's on my

way back from the gym.

Thinking back fondly

to the days when I could eat

pot pie at midnight.

Spinning endlessly.

Such pain! Such sweat! Such chafing!

I'd rather not, thanks.

Yoga clears your mind,

strengthens your soul, and heals you

leaving you crippled.

Treading on the mill,

I am just like the hamster,

hoofing for some grains.

Training wheels, training

bras, and personal trainers.

The Cycle of Life.

Mirrors everywhere—

I am inspired to lose weight.

Or hide in the back.

Contorted, I am

suddenly aware that I

need a pedicure.

Often I run to

catch the bus or the subway.

Isn't that enough?

The pool at the Y.

I hold my nose and jump in.

Sound of tidal wave.

THE NOT SO NOBLE TRUTH: MEDITATIONS ON JEALOUSY

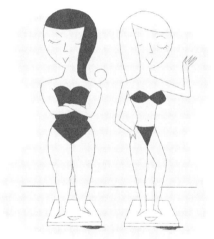

From time to time, as we bush-
whack our way to Thin, many of
us fall prey to petty feelings of
Jealousy, the third of the Four Evil
No-no's. Sadly, fashion and fitness

magazines don't help us, despite their alluring promises of Top Ten Tummy-Reduction Tips, E-Z Makeovers, and the like, for they serve only to remind us of our shortcomings. Assaulted on a near-daily basis by glossy photographs of Cameron Diaz and Jennifer Aniston shamelessly exposing their taut, flawless selves in skimpy low-riders and halter tops, we start to lose hope. Matters only worsen when we notice that some of our fellow travelers to the Land of Thin seem to be riding in the fast lane—perhaps shedding as many as five to ten pounds per week—while the rest of us flounder at the rest stop of life, where Temptation, Sloth, and Weakness reign supreme.

Ertha was at her best when counseling us about the dangers of Jealousy. Her strategy consisted primarily of bolstering everyone's self-image. When that didn't work, she would offer mind-boggling parables or personal anecdotes in order to distract us from our feelings of inadequacy. Her last-ditch effort was to remind us that, throughout history—starting with the gods and goddesses of Olympus and continuing right on to the Brad Pitts and Julia Robertses of Rodeo Drive—the "Beautiful People" have often turned out to be desperately unhappy and insecure beneath their airbrushed happy masks.

THINSPIRATION

"One good turnover deserves another."

Stuck between the rocks,

Jason and the Argonauts

Lost some weight at last!

Tantalus reaches.

He cannot grasp the fruit. Good!

He was out of Points.

Have you seen Venus

lately? I think she must have

had some ribs removed.

Achilles is thin.

A man with severed tendon

Cannot reach the fridge.

Consider Helen,

whose face launched all that troubl

Better to be plain.

The wind blows. A twig

scuttles past us on the walk.

Or was that Kate Moss?

Walking past Prada,

I wonder, who can wear such

skimpy little clothes?

With a private cook

and a personal trainer,

I would lose weight, too.

I see Calista

and I think it's a pity

no one feeds the girl.

Headline from London:

"The Duchess of York Spotted—

Eating Buttered Scones!"

Think of their savings!

Suits for Jen and Brad made from

just one yard of cloth!

If cameras add weight,

it's a wonder Courteney Cox

has the strength to stand.

The Shroud of Turin

gives way to the Rib of Cher.

The pilgrim's progress.

CONFUCIUS SAY: BEWARE THE FAD DIET TRAP!

A fter what seems like an eternity of slogging through the muddy, pothole-ridden road to Thin, it is not at all surprising that many of us begin to lose faith in our guide and contemplate setting out on our own. After all, at this point in our journey, we may be feeling tired and demoralized, perhaps even angry about the fact that we've schlepped faithfully to our weekly meetings with Ertha for the past several months and lost only half a pound. The skimpy bathing suit that we bought in an optimistic moment last March is still in the dresser drawer, tags intact. We have hit rock bottom and are therefore particularly vulnerable to Weakness (the most troubling of the Four Evil No-no's) and its depraved henchman, the Fad Diet.

Weakness typically lies in wait at the checkout lines, ready to ambush. Alone in the hostile landscape of the grocery store, we find ourselves attracted to these popular magazines as they taunt us over the heaping mounds of cookies, candies, and pudding snak-paks that spill out of our carts.

Ertha, blessed with the great intuition of a true master, anticipated the attack of Weakness and tried to ready us for the challenge, pointing out the

THINSPIRATION

"The worst things in life are fat-free."

inherent contradictions hidden in every quick-fix diet trap. Like the Devil to Dr. Faust, fad diets promise the impossible—that we'll lose weight while eating nothing but buttery, cheese-filled omelettes, thick slabs of bacon, and piles of beef jerky, or that we can maintain our sanity and our friends while eating startling amounts of cabbage or grapefruit, day in and day out. Until we accept that it simply cannot be that easy, we might as well forget about wearing that tiny little bikini, because we will never know the pleasures that await us in the Land of Thin.

Headline from L.A.:

"New Celebrity Diet—

Hooked on Colonics!"

Breaking bread in good

conscience becomes difficult.

One piece: twenty carbs.

Surrounded by crushed

Slim-Fast cans and Dexatrim.

The diet junkie.

I spent the morning

in a zone of perfection,

shelling one almond.

Too much cabbage makes

a person unpopular.

Just think about it.

The doctor's orders:

Bacon and eggs twice a day.

Avoid exercise.

Make that fruit salad

last a whole week. Diet,

Beverly Hills style.

Tasty pink grapefruit—

significantly less so

after the eighth day.

"Has it come to this?"

I cry, tearing greedily

into the jerky.

Just ask Al Roker

what to do if you've grown tired

of those Slim-Fast shakes.

Two parts protein, one

part fat. Fourteen days of fun.

The Scarsdale Diet.

"Throw off your fat dress!"

Lynn Redgrave encouraged us.

What, then, do I wear?

Curl into a ball

and refuse to eat for days.

The Gandhi Diet.

My shrink says I don't

need Susan Powter to stop

the insanity.

Wondering when the

ketosis will kick in, I

reach for the ham hock.

Large block of tofu.

Rosemary, sprig of parsley.

The Ornish "game hen."

In the old orchard,

standing under the fruit trees.

Points hang low and ripe.

WHEN HUNGRY, I EAT: PACKING A HEALTHY BENTO BOX FOR THE JOURNEY

If there's one lesson to be learned, it's that you can't trust everything you read. One day we're told that a healthy diet includes loads of protein and no bread or pasta. The next day we're told never to mix dairy with grains. Then we learn that fat is good and fruit is bad. Bewildered and a bit light-headed from the nutritional roller coaster we've been riding, we give up, refusing to empty our cupboards of the offending items du jour as we have done in the past.

Teetering on the edge of sanity (and, perhaps, just moments away from diabetic coma, heart failure, galloping obesity, hypoglycemia, simple chronic halitosis, or worse), we swallow a tasteless slice of humble pie and crawl back to Ertha.

Never one to judge, Ertha welcomed us back into the fold, her

THINSPIRATION

"Waste not, want not.

Mind if I finish that?"

beatific smile offering solace as we stepped down from the scales in defeat. Looking out at our bloated faces, she sensed that it was finally time to impart her valuable healthful-eating tips, those fat-free nuggets of wisdom I will forever carry with me in my purse.

Convert one slice of pizza into two with a single stroke of the knife! Turn an uneventful glass of water into a delightfully refreshing treat with nothing but a slice of lemon and a pack of Equal! Prolong the pleasure of fat-free ice cream by trading in your trowels for demi-tasse spoons! Who knew that the whole secret to Thin was contained in a deceptively simple cause-and-effect formula: (1) fat-free food is tasteless, (2) we will eat less of it because it's tasteless, and (3) eventu-ally, we will lose weight because we're not eating!

Finally, we see the Land of Thin glimmering like a beacon on the horizon!

Sugar-free Jell-O

slides quickly to the stomach.

Hunger rages on.

Sad realization:

Fat-free foods never taste as

good as fat-filled ones.

How can I trust the

Gorton's fisherman after

reading that label?

Crispy brown Wasa,

with its corrugated folds,

not unlike cardboard.

Olestra chips with

a Pepto-Bismol chaser.

The fun never ends.

The vegan picnic:

cheeseless cheese on breadless bread.

Splenda in the grass.

Molly McButter's

a nice girl (though some people

say she's a phony).

Food tastes much better

with a dash of wheat germ flakes.

Or so they tell us.

Slivers of raw fish

laid out on a wooden plank.

You call this dinner?

Beer: good for your hair,

yet so bad for your waistline.

Life's cruel paradox.

Looking at the wheat

rippling in the summer breeze,

I feel regular.

From the sundae to

the fruit salad. Banana,

the versatile fruit.

Thank you, Jack La Lanne,

for introducing some style

to the world of juice.

The one thing that you

can eat with abandon while

still losing weight. Prunes.

I'll have the bacon,

lettuce, and tomato, please.

Without the bacon.

After eating the

whole box, I am still hungry.

Smart Ones. Not so smart.

ENLIGHTENUPMENT:
CLAWING OUR WAY
TO THIN

Even though Ertha far outpaced us mere mortals in the race to Enlightenupment, she understood that not everyone could, or wanted to, keep up. Some of us make it to Thin only to find that it just isn't all that it was promised to be. Others of us, after spending months in the trenches, may decide that we simply cannot make the sacrifices needed to gain entry to that rarefied land. A lucky few might even discover that happiness (preferably in the form of fondue) is more important than looking like Lara Flynn Boyle.

Fear not! Whatever your motivation, or lack thereof, you should not despair over your inability to make it all the way to the end of the path. We learned that, even in defeat, we can count on Ertha's valuable pearls of wisdom (and, if worn correctly,

T H I N S P I R A T I O N

"A waist is a terrible thing to mind."

they can hide an unsightly double chin). Thanks to more forgiving fabrics, vertical stripes, and exciting new confidential outpatient procedures, Ertha showed us that you can manage to look like you made it to Thin even if you never left the comfort of your own, well-stocked kitchen.

And if that doesn't do it, you can always try rationalization. It works for me.

THINSPIRATION

"You can't take it with you when you die,

so you might as well eat it."

Let haiku lead you

out of Hellfatdarkness. Run!

To the Land of Thin.

Here's a diet tip:

Surround yourself with people

who weigh more than you.

Here's another tip:

Surround yourself with people

who have poor vision.

See smiling Buddha.

Popular, happy, and fat.

Pass the Krispy Kremes.

"Maybe tomorrow,"

she said, dipping her spoon deep

into the carton.

We shall overcome.

If we don't, there are always

elastic waistbands.

Chic jeans come in so many shapes and sizes, I don't need to lose weight!

Tying my laces,

I feel profoundly grateful.

Thank you, stretch denim.

Rubens loved the gals

with plenty of hips and thighs.

Down with modern art!!

Pears are so lovely,

round, and succulent. No harm

in looking like one.

Thanks to that bypass,

you'll be a cheap date at the

tapas restaurant.

People always say,

"Never trust a skinny cook."

Why should I argue?

So I look like the

women Botero painted?

Everyone loves them!

Providing comfort

since the dawn of high-fat food.

The humble muumuu.

Ten pounds of sausage

in a sleek, five-pound casing.

The body slimmer.

4/3/23 JK
9/24